Mrs

Swamp Life

by Kristin Cashore

PEARSON
Scott
Foresman

DK

What You Already Know

A habitat is a place where animals and plants live. A habitat has air, food, water, and shelter.

A forest is a habitat. A forest has many trees and other plants. The forest has food, water, and sunlight for plants and animals.

An ocean is a habitat. An ocean has salt water. Plants and animals live in the ocean.

A forest habitat

A desert is a habitat. A desert is dry. It does not rain much. Deserts have lots of sunlight. Some deserts are hot during the day. Many plants and animals live in the desert.

A wetland is a habitat. A wetland has a lot of water. One kind of wetland is a swamp. Plants and animals live in wetland habitats.

Plants and animals live in many different habitats. In this book you will learn about swamps. You will learn about the plants and animals that call the swamp their home.

A swamp habitat

Life in a Swamp

A swamp is a wet place. Swamps are full of water. Sometimes a swamp looks like a lake with trees and plants growing in it. There are swamps all over the world.

The soil in a swamp is waterlogged. This means that the soil is always very wet. There is a lot of mud.

A swamp has many kinds of plants. Many animals live in the swamp too. Some animals live in the water. Some animals climb in the trees.

Swamps are wet habitats.
Swamps are full of life.

5

Plants

Many kinds of plants grow in swamps. Cypress trees grow in the water. The trunks are very wide at the bottom. They have long roots. Part of the roots grow on top of the water. The roots grab the wet dirt.

Cypress trees

Mangrove trees

Mangrove trees also grow in the water. These trees can look like they are walking in the water.

Trees are important to life in a swamp. Animals eat their leaves. Trees give food and shelter to animals in the swamp.

Some plants need a lot of water.
These plants grow well in swamps.
   The water hyacinth is a swamp plant.
It floats on the water. It has big blue
flowers. It can be as tall as a kitchen stove!
   Water lettuce is also a floating plant.
It has big green leaves.

Mangrove plant

Spiny-bellied orb weaver

Many animals live near swamp plants. The plants give these animals food and shelter.

The spiny-bellied orb weaver is a spider that lives in swamps. Guess how this spider gets its name? It has ten spines on its belly.

Some kinds of apple snail are very big. They can be as long as a pen!

Mangrove leaves

Water hyacinth

Water lettuce

Apple snail

9

In the Water

Some swamp animals swim in the water. Sometimes these animals rest at the edge of the water. Turtles, snakes, lizards, caimans, and alligators swim in swamp water.

Most of this caiman is under the water. Its eyes stay on top of the water to see.

Caiman

A caiman looks like an alligator. But it has a bump on top of its nose. It also has thick skin on its belly.

American alligator

Alligators and caimans look like logs when they are in the water. This helps them catch prey. They can be very dangerous!

Garter snake

In the Trees

Animals in swamps live in the water. They also live in the trees.

A green tree frog climbs and rests in swamp trees.

A bobcat is a kind of cat. It has long legs and a short tail. Bobcats swim and climb well. A swamp is a good home for them.

Green tree frog

Bobcat

Raccoons

**Raccoons find the food and shelter
they need in swamps.**

A raccoon looks like it is wearing a black mask. It also has black stripes on its tail. Raccoons eat animals and plants. They climb well in the trees of swamps. Trees are home to many swamp animals!

Birds

Many birds live in swamps. A lot of swamp birds wade in the water. They are called wading birds.

Wading birds have long legs and necks. They look for food in the water. Their toes are long and spread out. This helps them stand on wet ground. Wading birds eat animals like fish and insects.

Flamingos are wading birds. They have webbed feet to help them stand in the mud.

Flamingos are bright pink.

Blue herons are also wading birds. They use their beaks to catch food. They can stand in the water or on the land.

Many plants and animals have special parts that help them live in these wet places. These plants and animals make up a swamp habitat.

Blue heron

Glossary

dangerous	not safe
float	stay on top of water
prey	an animal that is the food of another animal
swamp	wet, soft land
wading	walking in the water
waterlogged	full of water